NON-TECHI GUIDE
TO
ARTIFICIAL INTELLIGENCE

Breaking Down AI for Beginners

AMANDA FLEISH

Amanda Fleish

DEDICATION

To those who dedicate their lives to understanding, supporting, and empowering others—Your patience, compassion, and unwavering commitment make the world a better place.

And to my family and friends, whose encouragement and belief in me fuel my passion for writing—thank you for always being by my side.

Amanda Fleish

PREFACE

Welcome to the *Non-Techi Guide to Artificial Intelligence: Breaking Down AI for Beginners*. If you've ever felt overwhelmed or unsure about the world of artificial intelligence, this book is for you. With AI now part of our everyday lives—from voice assistants like Siri to smart home devices to tools that help us work more efficiently—understanding how to use these technologies can seem daunting, especially if you've never explored them. But don't worry! This book is designed to help you get up to speed with AI in the simplest, most approachable way possible.

Whether you've never used AI or feel behind the curve, this guide will walk you through everything you need to know. We'll break down complicated concepts and show you how to use AI to enhance your life, whether by helping you stay organized, be more productive, or simply have a little more fun with technology.

As you progress through the chapters, you'll understand how AI works, how to use different AI tools, and how to take advantage of their growing capabilities. No technical background is needed—this guide is for anyone, no matter your level of experience with technology.

Amanda Fleish

DISCLAIMER

Please note that any apps or AI tools mentioned in this book are simply suggestions based on their functionality and usefulness for beginners. *I do not receive compensation, commission, or endorsements for recommending them.* The goal is to provide helpful resources to improve your understanding of AI and how it can work for you. I encourage you to explore these options and choose the best fit for your needs. This book is intended as an introductory guide to artificial intelligence (AI) tools and applications for beginners. The information provided is for educational and informational purposes only and should not be considered professional, financial, or technical advice. Readers should actively participate in their learning journey by conducting research and using discretion when adopting AI tools or technologies.

The inclusion of specific AI tools is based on their current availability and relevance at the time of writing. It's important to note that the features, pricing, and accessibility of these tools may change over time, and I make no guarantees regarding their continued availability or functionality.

It's important to note that mentioning any product, company, or service in this book does not imply endorsement. The decision to use these tools is entirely at the reader's discretion. I do not take responsibility for any outcomes, experiences, or decisions based on the information in this book.

Amanda Fleish

Amanda Fleish

TABLE OF CONTENTS

INTRODUCTION

If you've ever felt overwhelmed or confused when people talk about artificial intelligence, you're not alone. The world of AI might seem like a distant, futuristic concept, but the truth is, it's already part of your everyday life, whether you realize it or not. AI is already making your life easier, from the voice assistants on your phone to the personalized recommendations you see online.

This book is for anyone who feels like the world of technology is a bit too complicated to dive into—especially when it comes to AI. You might have heard about AI on the news or seen it in movies and probably know more than you think. Even if you're unsure how it works or why it's essential, don't worry; you're in the right place!

This guide is designed to make AI easy to understand. We'll break down AI in the simplest, most straightforward way possible, using everyday language and no tech jargon. We'll talk about what AI is, how it affects your day-to-day life, and how you can use it to your advantage—whether for work, learning, or just having fun. And we'll walk you through everything step by step.

You might be surprised at how much you're already interacting with AI! From voice assistants like Siri and Alexa to the personalized recommendations you see online, AI is already helping you in more ways than you realize. This book aims to help you understand AI and see how it can make your life easier, more productive, and even more fun.

By the end of this book, you'll have a solid understanding of what AI is, how it works, and how you can use it—even if you've never considered yourself "tech-savvy." You've made a great decision to learn about AI!

DEMYSTIFYING AI

When you hear the term "artificial intelligence" or "AI," what comes to mind? Maybe you picture a robot like the ones in science fiction movies or a supercomputer making decisions all on its own. While those ideas aren't far off in the future, AI today is much simpler and is already part of your daily life in ways you may not even realize. And the best part? It's not as complex as it may seem. AI is accessible and understandable, even for those new to the concept.

Artificial intelligence (AI) refers to the capability of a computer or machine to think and learn like humans. The key concept here is "learning." Just as humans acquire new knowledge through practice or study, AI learns by analyzing data. It can recognize patterns, make predictions, and solve problems based on the information it receives. However, it's important to note that AI does not possess feelings or process thoughts like people do. Instead, it uses data to identify the best or most helpful solutions.

For example, think about what happens when you search for something on Google. The search results are based on AI that understands your question and matches it with the most relevant pages online. Or when you use your smartphone's voice assistant, like Siri or Alexa. These assistants are powered by AI, which helps them understand what you're saying and respond in a way that makes sense. They don't have emotions or personal opinions. Still, they're good at understanding patterns in language so that they can give you helpful answers.

So, why does AI matter to you? Because it already works in the background of many things you do daily. It's helping you find what you need online, recommending the next movie you should watch, or even telling you the quickest route to work. AI is changing how we live, work, and interact with the world around us—and it's happening right now! And the best part? It's here to make your life easier, not harder.

AI is all around us: It's in the apps we use, the websites we visit, and the devices we rely on. But just because it's all around us doesn't mean we must be scared. AI is here to make things easier for us, not harder. You don't need to become an expert to understand how AI works or how it can benefit you. All you need is the curiosity to learn more about it, and that's precisely what we will do in this book.

In the next chapter, we'll dive deeper into how AI works—and we'll keep it simple. You'll see that learning about AI doesn't have to be as complicated as it sounds. It's all about understanding the basics and taking things one step at a time. With curiosity and proper guidance, you'll find that understanding AI is well within your reach.

HOW AI WORKS (SIMPLIFIED)

If AI is so intelligent, you might wonder, how does it work? The good news is that you don't need to be a tech expert to understand the basics.

Let's break it down step by step. Imagine you're teaching a child how to ride a bike. At first, the child might not know how to balance or steer. But as they practice, they learn from their mistakes and improve. The more they practice, the easier it becomes. AI works similarly. Instead of a child, it's a computer or a machine; instead of a bike, it's learning from data.

In simple terms, AI learns by analyzing lots of information—often called data—and then figuring out patterns. For example, if you wanted AI to recognize pictures of cats, you'd show it thousands of photos labeled "cat" and "not cat." The AI doesn't know what a cat is at first. But over time, it starts recognizing features like pointy ears, whiskers, and furry bodies. The more pictures it sees, the better it gets at identifying cats. Eventually, it can look at a new picture and say, "That's a cat," even if it's never seen that exact photo before.

This process is called machine learning, the most common way AI works. It's like teaching someone a skill through repetition and practice. The more the AI practices with data, the brighter it becomes.

Amanda Fleish

A Peek Inside the AI Brain: Neural Networks

You've probably heard the term "neural network" in the context of AI. Sounds complicated, right? Let's simplify it.

Think of a neural network as interconnected "neurons," similar to how our brains work. But instead of being made of cells, these "neurons" are just mathematical formulas or computer programs that help AI process information. They're organized in layers, and each layer looks at different parts of the data. The more layers there are, the more complex the decisions AI can make.

When you show AI an image, each layer of the neural network breaks it down bit by bit—one layer might look at the colors, another might focus on shapes, and another might focus on textures. In the end, it all comes together to make a decision. So, when you see a picture of a cat, the AI uses all these layers of analysis to guess what it is.

The Power of Data: How AI Learns

The key to AI's ability to "learn" is the data it uses. The more data it gets, the brighter it can become. Think of data like the ingredients in a recipe. If you have high-quality ingredients (sound data), you can make a delicious meal (accurate results). But the meal won't turn out well if your ingredients aren't fresh or are mixed incorrectly (poor data).

For example, when AI helps doctors diagnose diseases, it uses medical data—like patient records, images, and test results—to make predictions. The more accurate and diverse the data, the more valuable the AI will be.

A Simple Example of AI Learning

Let's take a simple example: an AI that helps recommend movies. Imagine you watch a few action movies, and the AI starts noticing a pattern—it sees that you often watch fast-paced, adventure-filled films. Based on this data, the AI might suggest similar movies you haven't watched yet.

The more you watch, the better the recommendations because AI will learn your preferences over time.

That's the beauty of machine learning. It allows AI to improve as it continuously acquires more data. So, if you like action movies today but start watching comedies tomorrow, the AI will notice the change and adjust its recommendations accordingly.

So, AI doesn't have a mind of its own—it simply looks at patterns and uses data to make predictions or decisions. It doesn't understand the world like a person does. Still, it's excellent at identifying patterns in vast amounts of information faster than any human could.

In the next chapter, we'll look at how AI is already helping you in your daily life, often without you even realizing it. Whether it's the apps you use, the websites you visit, or the devices you interact with, AI is quietly working behind the scenes to make things easier.

NOTES

AI IN YOUR EVERYDAY LIFE

If you've ever used a smartphone, browsed the internet, or watched a movie recommendation, you've already encountered AI. It might not have seemed like AI then, but it's quietly working behind the scenes to make your life more convenient, faster, and enjoyable.

This chapter will explore how AI seamlessly integrates into your daily routine—often without you even realizing it!

AI in Your Smartphone

Let's start with your smartphone. Suppose you use a phone with a virtual assistant like Siri (Apple) or Google Assistant. In that case, you use AI every time you ask it a question or command it. You might say, "Hey, Siri, what's the weather today?" or "Google, set an alarm for 7 a.m." These voice assistants use AI to understand your words, figure out what you mean, and give you a helpful response.

But it doesn't stop there. AI also helps organize your photos, recommend music, and even make typing faster with predictive text. It can learn how you speak, the people you talk to, and the places you visit, getting better at assisting you the more you use it. This makes your experience more personalized and tailored to your needs.

AI in Social Media

Have you ever wondered how Facebook, Instagram, or YouTube always seem to know what you like? That's AI at work. These platforms use AI to analyze your activity—such as the posts you want, the videos you watch, and the people you follow—and then suggest new content based on your interests.

For example, suppose you spend a lot of time watching cooking videos on YouTube. The AI will notice that and suggest more cooking-related content in that case. Or, if you like photos of your friends on Facebook, the AI will show you more posts from them in your feed. The more you interact with these platforms, the better the AI gets at personalizing your experience.

AI in Shopping

Next time you're online shopping, take a moment to notice the recommendations you see. Whether shopping on Amazon, Etsy, or any other online store, AI is working hard to suggest items you might like. It looks at your past purchases, what you've viewed, and what others are buying to give you tailored suggestions.

Ever seen those "Customers who bought this also bought…" sections on websites? That's AI at work, analyzing buying patterns to help you discover new products. It's like having a personal shopping assistant that learns your preferences over time.

AI in Navigation

If you've ever used Google Maps or Waze to get directions, you've used AI to help you navigate the roads. These apps use AI to analyze real-time traffic data, weather conditions, and accidents, giving you the best route to your destination. And suppose there's an unexpected traffic jam or roadblock. In that case, the AI will automatically find a faster way for you to get there.

It doesn't stop at driving, either. Public transportation apps also use AI to provide accurate schedules, track buses or trains in real time, and suggest the quickest routes to your destination.

AI in Entertainment

Have you ever gotten hooked on a TV show or movie recommended by Netflix, Hulu, or Amazon Prime? AI is behind these recommendations, too. These streaming services use AI to track your viewing habits and suggest movies and shows based on your previous watch.

But it's not just about recommendations. AI also powers features like automatic subtitles, speech recognition, and video editing. When you watch a show, the captions you see are often generated by AI that can automatically recognize the dialogue and translate it into text. Even when scrolling through channels, AI might be helping you discover the perfect show by analyzing ratings, preferences, and trending topics.

AI in Smart Homes

Suppose you have a smart home device like Amazon Alexa, Google Home, or a smart thermostat. In that case, you're already interacting with

AI. These devices can learn your habits and adjust things like lighting and temperature, and they can even play music based on your preferences.

For example, a smart thermostat can learn your schedule and adjust the temperature automatically to save energy when you're not at home. It learns your patterns and adjusts accordingly to make your home more comfortable without thinking about it.

AI in Health and Fitness

AI is also impacting health and fitness. Many fitness trackers and health apps use AI to analyze your activity and suggest improvements. If you use an app like MyFitnessPal or Fitbit, AI can track your steps, workouts, and food intake to help you reach your health goals.

Some AI-powered devices can even monitor your heart rate or sleep patterns and alert you if something seems off. It's like having a personal health coach on your wrist, helping you stay healthy and active.

As you can see, AI is already everywhere. From the apps on your phone to the recommendations you get online, AI is quietly working behind the scenes to make your life smoother, faster, and more personalized. It doesn't always scream, "I'm AI!" but trust me, it's there, making your day easier.

And the best part? You don't need to be a tech expert to take advantage of AI. In fact, by the time you finish this book, you'll be able to use AI tools and understand how they can make your life better.

In the next chapter, we'll dive deeper into the different types of AI—what they can do and why they're essential for the future. But for now, take a moment to think about all the ways AI is already working for you. Pretty amazing, right?

THE DIFFERENT TYPES OF AI

In this chapter, we'll look at the main types of AI, how they differ, and why they matter to you daily. Don't worry—this will be straightforward to grasp, and practical knowledge can enhance your understanding of the technology you use.

Narrow AI vs. General AI

When discussing AI, you first need to understand the difference between Narrow AI (sometimes called Weak AI) and General AI (also called Strong AI). These terms might sound complicated, but they're not as tricky as they seem. This information is accessible to everyone, and we'll break it down in a way that's easy to understand.

Narrow AI is the type of AI we have today. It's designed to do one specific task well. Narrow AI is like a specialist—it's great at solving one problem but can't do anything outside of that. For example, voice assistants like Siri or Google Assistant are forms of Narrow AI. They can help you set alarms, check the weather, or find nearby restaurants, but they'd struggle if you asked them to solve a complex math problem or write an essay.

Other examples of Narrow AI include:

- Spam filters in your email: They're designed to recognize and block unwanted messages.

- Netflix and Amazon have recommendation systems. These systems suggest movies or products based on your watch or purchase.

- Face recognition on your phone: It helps unlock your phone by recognizing your face.

The key to Narrow AI is that it is task-specific. It doesn't "think" beyond what it's programmed to do but does that one thing well.

General AI, on the other hand, is the type of AI you often see in science fiction movies. This would be an AI that can understand and learn any intellectual task that a human can do. Imagine a robot that can learn languages, play chess, solve complex problems, and even create art. We don't have General AI yet, but it's still something researchers are working on. But Narrow AI? That's already here and making a significant impact in our daily lives.

The Power of Machine Learning

Most AI you interact with today is powered by machine learning, which teaches computers to recognize patterns and make data-based decisions. It's a key part of Narrow AI and how devices and apps get smarter over time.

With machine learning, AI doesn't need to be explicitly programmed with every rule or decision. Instead, it can "learn" from data and improve its performance on its own. The more data it gets, the better it gets at making predictions or completing tasks.

For example, if you're using a navigation app like Google Maps, it uses machine learning to improve its routes. The more people use it, the better it predicts traffic patterns and offers faster routes. It learns from millions of drivers' data to make real-time decisions.

Deep Learning: The Next Step Up

You may have heard about deep learning in the context of AI. It's a subset of machine learning where things get even more advanced. Deep learning mimics how our brains work, using artificial neural networks with many layers (hence the term "deep"). These networks can process vast amounts of data, recognize more complex patterns, and perform tasks like image or speech recognition.

For instance, artificial intelligence utilized in autonomous vehicles depends on deep learning to identify objects on the roadway, such as other vehicles, pedestrians, and traffic signals. It can analyze a large volume of visual data instantly, enabling rapid decisions, such as when to halt or make a turn. Although deep learning is an incredibly effective tool, it remains a component of Narrow AI.

What About Artificial General Intelligence (AGI)?

You might have heard about Artificial General Intelligence (AGI), the idea of an AI that can perform any task a human brain can do. AGI would be capable of learning and reasoning across various areas, just like a person. It could solve problems, learn languages, think critically, and be creative.

We haven't arrived there yet. AGI is still theoretical, and scientists are working hard to figure out how to create such an intelligent system. While Narrow AI and machine learning are powerful tools, AGI is still in the distant future. For now, we'll continue to see AI used in specific, specialized ways—like helping with recommendations, recognizing faces, or automating tasks.

Why Does This Matter to You?

So, why should you care about the difference between Narrow AI, General AI, and deep learning? Understanding these concepts will help you see where AI is heading and how it impacts your life. Right now, you're primarily interacting with Narrow AI, and you'll likely continue to see more AI-powered tools around you—whether it's for personal use, work, or even in the health field.

Narrow AI is already powerful enough to improve daily life through personalized recommendations, faster navigation, or more brilliant virtual assistants. Even though AGI is a long way off, staying curious and open to how AI might evolve is essential. AI's potential to revolutionize our lives is vast, and understanding its different types can help us embrace this future with optimism.

In the next chapter, we'll examine how AI is used in the workplace, how it's changing industries, and what jobs people do with AI's help.

AI IN THE WORKPLACE

Artificial intelligence is enhancing our everyday convenience and revolutionizing the workplace. Whether you are in an office, working remotely, or employed in a factory, AI is redefining various industries and individuals' roles. This section will examine the applications of AI across different work settings and its impact on efficiency, creativity, and productivity.

Automating Repetitive Tasks

One of the most common uses of AI in the workplace today is liberating professionals from the burden of automating repetitive tasks. Just imagine the relief from all the small tasks you do throughout the day that are necessary but not particularly exciting. AI can take over these repetitive tasks, freeing time for employees to focus on more critical, creative, or strategic work, making you feel more liberated and productive.

AI can take over these repetitive tasks, freeing employees to focus on more critical, creative, or strategic work. For example, in an office setting, chatbots powered by AI can answer common customer service questions, schedule appointments, or even manage bookings. This allows customer service representatives to spend more time solving complex issues that require human understanding.

Robotic Process Automation (RPA) is another example. AI can handle tasks like processing invoices, verifying data, or checking for errors in the finance, healthcare, and insurance industries. It doesn't get tired, works faster than a human, and reduces the chances of making mistakes. The result? More time for employees to engage in higher-level work that drives innovation.

AI in Customer Service

AI also plays a significant role in customer service. Many companies use AI-powered chatbots to assist customers online. These bots can help customers find information, place orders, or troubleshoot problems.

Take a look at the website of any major retailer. There's a good chance they offer a chatbot to help you with your purchase, track your order, or answer questions about a product. These bots use natural language processing (NLP), a type of AI, to understand your questions and give appropriate responses.

The beauty of AI in customer service is that it can work 24/7. So even if it's 3 a.m. and you have a question, AI is ready to assist, making you feel reassured and supported. For companies, AI chatbots reduce the need for live agents, allowing human workers to focus on more complex customer issues that require a personal touch.

AI in Healthcare

AI is making significant advancements in healthcare, assisting doctors and nurses in providing better patient care. For example, AI systems can analyze medical images like X-rays and MRIs to help doctors detect potential issues like tumors or fractures. These AI tools operate at incredible speeds, often identifying problems that human eyes may overlook.

Moreover, AI is not limited to diagnosis. It can help healthcare providers monitor patients' vital signs, predict potential health risks, and even recommend treatments based on their medical history. This technology enables doctors to make more informed decisions and improves patient outcomes.

AI-powered health apps can also help patients manage chronic conditions. For example, AI tools can remind patients to take their medications or track their symptoms, offering insights into their health over time.

AI in Marketing and Advertising

In marketing, AI transforms how companies reach and engage with their customers. AI-powered systems can analyze customer behavior, predict trends, and create personalized advertisements that are more likely to catch a person's attention. Think of it like a personal shopper—AI can recommend products based on your preferences, purchases, and browsing history.

For example, online shopping platforms like Amazon or Netflix use AI to suggest items or movies you might like. They look at what you've viewed or bought before and suggest similar products, making the shopping experience more personal and convenient.

In advertising, AI helps companies create more targeted and effective campaigns. AI tools can analyze customer data to determine the best time, platform, and messaging for advertisements, ensuring marketing dollars are spent more efficiently.

Amanda Fleish

AI in Human Resources

Another area where AI is making waves is in Human Resources (HR). Hiring can be a lengthy, complex process, but AI is helping streamline it. AI-powered tools can screen resumes, match candidates to job descriptions, and even conduct initial interviews via chatbots. This allows HR departments should focus on the most promising candidates and save time on the administrative side.

AI can also help with employee training. Virtual training assistants powered by AI can deliver customized training programs to employees, helping them develop new skills or improve existing ones. These programs can adapt to each employee's pace, ensuring that training is as practical as possible.

AI in Creative Industries

You might wonder if AI can be creative. The answer is yes. Although AI excels in tasks that involve analysis and repetition, it is also beginning to penetrate creative domains such as writing, art, and music.

AI applications are utilized for crafting news articles, producing music, and generating visual artwork. For instance, specific AI programs can create sports summaries or financial news pieces by interpreting data and transforming it into coherent content. Additionally, AI has produced artwork influenced by existing styles, presenting new opportunities for artists and designers.

AI has been used to compose original pieces by analyzing thousands of songs across different genres. It can help musicians create new ideas or write full compositions based on specific moods or themes.

While AI will not replace human creativity, it's a great tool for sparking ideas, improving workflow, and enhancing creativity in many industries. AI's potential to enhance creativity is inspiring. It offers new possibilities for artists, designers, and professionals across various industries, making you feel inspired and optimistic about the future of work.

What Does This All Mean for You?

While AI is a powerful tool, it's important to note that it's not a panacea. It's not here to take your career but to help make your work easier, faster, and more efficient. However, there are tasks that AI may not be able to handle as effectively as humans, especially those that require emotional intelligence, complex problem-solving, or creativity.

With the increasing integration of AI in the workplace, some job roles may evolve or change. For example, if you work in customer service, AI-powered chatbots might handle basic inquiries, allowing you to focus on solving more complex problems. In marketing, AI tools could help you design more effective campaigns. AI could help you make more accurate diagnoses and provide better healthcare. However, it's important to note that AI is not here to replace human workers but to augment their capabilities and make their jobs more efficient.

The key takeaway? AI is not something to fear—it's a tool that can make your job easier and allow you to do more meaningful work.

In the upcoming chapter, we will explore strategies for leveraging AI to enhance productivity—be it in work, study, or simply maintaining organization. AI is a resource accessible to all, regardless of career field.

THOUGHTS SO FAR

_____

_____

_____

_____

_____

_____

_____

_____

_____

_____

_____

_____

_____

_____

_____

_____

_____

_____

BOOSTING YOUR PRODUCTIVITY

You're not alone if you feel there's never enough time in the day. Whether juggling work, family, or personal projects, staying on top of everything can be overwhelming. Luckily, AI is here to help you boost your productivity, stay organized, and make the most of your time. However, considering the potential ethical implications of AI use, such as privacy concerns or job displacement, is essential. This chapter will look at practical ways to use AI to improve your daily routine, keep your tasks organized, and get more done in less time while considering these broader societal implications.

AI-Powered Personal Assistants

You've probably heard of virtual assistants like Siri, Google Assistant, or Alexa. These AI-powered tools can help you stay on top of your day by managing your calendar, setting reminders, and answering quick questions. But they can do so much more.

For example:

- You can ask your assistant to add events to your calendar or remind you of upcoming meetings.

- You can set timers for tasks like cooking or working in focused intervals.

- You can have your assistant send messages, make phone calls, or even play your favorite music to help you focus.

AI-powered personal assistants are designed to reduce mental clutter by handling small tasks and allowing you to focus on the big stuff. They're like having a personal secretary who's always available to help, making your tasks more manageable and you feel more at ease.

AI to Manage Your Time

One of the biggest challenges of being productive is managing your time effectively. Thankfully, AI tools are here to help you stay organized and use your time wisely. For instance, AI-powered calendar apps can help you schedule appointments, plan your day, and suggest optimal times for meetings or tasks based on your availability.

Some AI apps, like Clockwise or Motion, even optimize your calendar by adjusting events automatically, ensuring you have time for essential tasks without overloading your schedule. These tools can also track how much time you spend on different activities and provide reports to help you understand where your time is going.

If you struggle with procrastination, AI apps like Focus@Will or Forest can help you stay focused by offering music or soundscapes designed to improve concentration. They block distractions and encourage you to work in focused bursts of time, making it easier to stay on track.

Automating Your Workflows

Countless small, repetitive tasks take up much of your time, but AI can help automate many. You can use workflow automation tools to streamline tasks and let AI do the heavy lifting.

For example, if you work with emails, AI tools like SaneBox or Clean Email can automatically sort your inbox, categorize messages, and even unsubscribe you from unwanted newsletters. These tools save you time by keeping your inbox neat and ensuring you only see what's important.

You can automate tasks between different apps using apps like Zapier or IFTTT (If This, Then That). For instance, you can set up an automation that saves all your email attachments to a cloud storage service or automatically posts your latest blog entry to social media. The possibilities are endless!

Automating repetitive tasks frees up time for more valuable activities, such as focusing on a big project, spending time with family, or even taking a break to recharge.

Using AI to Organize Your Tasks

Another great way AI can boost your productivity is by helping you stay organized. Instead of relying on paper to-do lists or trying to keep everything in your head, AI apps like Todoist, Trello, or Notion can help you organize your tasks, track your progress, and focus on what needs to be done.

These apps use AI to prioritize your tasks based on deadlines, importance, and the time you've set aside for each task. They can even suggest tasks to work on next based on your goals and the time available. These apps often integrate with your calendar and other tools to sync across platforms.

For example, suppose you're working on a project with multiple steps. In that case, you can break it down into smaller tasks within a project management app. The AI can then show you what needs to be done, when to start, and when you should aim to finish, keeping everything on track.

AI for Writing and Content Creation

If you create content—whether it's for work, a blog, or social media—AI can help speed up the process. Grammarly, for example, uses AI to check your writing for grammar, spelling, and style issues. It can even suggest ways to improve your writing and make it sound more professional.

Suppose you're struggling with writer's block. In that case, AI tools like Jasper (formerly Jarvis) or Copy.ai can help generate content ideas or even write entire blog posts, marketing copy, and social media content. These tools use AI to understand the type of content you want to create and help you get started with text that is ready to refine.

For those who need to design graphics or presentations, AI tools like Canva can help create professional-looking designs with minimal effort. Whether creating social media posts, posters, or infographics, AI in design software enables you to create polished visuals quickly.

AI for Managing Finances

Managing your finances can be stressful, but AI-powered apps can make it easier. Mint and YNAB (You Need a Budget) are examples of financial apps that use AI to track your spending, create budgets, and even offer financial advice. These apps analyze your spending patterns and help you make smarter decisions about saving and budgeting.

AI tools like Clearscore and Credit Karma can also help you monitor your credit score and alert you to any changes so you can stay on top of your financial health.

For people who invest, AI is even being used in robo-advisors to help manage investment portfolios. These tools use algorithms to suggest investments based on your risk tolerance, financial goals, and market trends, making it easier to grow your money with minimal effort.

The Future of Productivity and AI

As AI continues to improve, we can expect even more advanced productivity tools in the future. From AI-powered virtual assistants that understand your needs even better to advanced project management systems that automatically adjust schedules, the potential for AI to increase productivity is vast.

In the future, AI may even learn from your work habits and personal preferences, providing more personalized recommendations and assistance. Imagine an AI that knows when you're most productive, when to schedule breaks, and how to keep you focused and energized throughout the day. The potential for AI to enhance productivity is vast and exciting.

The key takeaway from this chapter is that AI can be a powerful ally in managing your time, staying organized, and automating tasks that take up too much of your day. By integrating AI into your routine, you'll be able to spend more time on what matters most and less time stressing over the details.

In the next chapter, we'll look at how you can use AI to learn new skills—whether for personal growth, career development, or just for fun.

YOUR PERSONAL LEARNING ASSISTANT

Have you ever wished you could learn something new but didn't know where to start or how to fit it into your busy schedule? The great news is that AI can help you learn new skills—whether you want to pick up a new hobby, improve at work, or even change careers. In this chapter, we'll explore how AI can be your personal learning assistant, offering benefits such as personalized learning paths, real-time feedback, and the ability to learn at your own pace, all of which can help you gain new knowledge and skills in an easy, personalized, and efficient way.

AI-Powered Learning Apps

Gone are the days of traditional classrooms being the only place to learn. Thanks to AI, countless learning apps can teach you anything from a new language to coding, cooking, or photography.

For example, Duolingo is an AI-powered language learning app that adapts to your skill level and learning pace. It uses algorithms to personalize lessons based on the areas where you need the most practice, providing you with a sense of support and guidance. If you're struggling with a particular set of words or grammar rules, Duolingo will adjust its lessons to help you improve in those areas, ensuring you're always on the right track.

Similarly, apps like Khan Academy and Coursera offer personalized learning experiences in subjects ranging from math and science to arts and humanities. These platforms use AI to track your progress, suggest relevant courses and provide tailored feedback, ensuring you learn quickly.

AI for Learning New Hobbies

Maybe you're not looking to learn a new language or take an online course but rather develop a hobby. AI can help with that, too! For example, if you've always wanted to learn to play the piano, apps like Simply Piano use AI to listen to your playing and provide instant feedback. It adapts to your skill level, guiding you from the basics to advanced techniques.

If you're interested in photography, AI-based apps like Photomath or Adobe Lightroom can help you improve your photography skills. AI analyzes your photos, suggesting adjustments to enhance lighting, color, or composition, helping you learn through real-time corrections.

For people interested in cooking, AI-powered apps like Yummly can recommend recipes based on what you already have in your kitchen. The app can also offer step-by-step instructions and tips based on your cooking style or dietary preferences. You can learn new cooking techniques without traditional cooking classes and discover new meals.

Personalized Learning Paths

One of the best things about AI is how it creates personalized learning experiences. Rather than a one-size-fits-all approach, AI can help customize your learning path, making the process more effective and enjoyable.

For example, suppose you're using an AI-powered fitness app like Freeletics. In that case, the app will create a workout plan tailored to your goals, whether you're trying to build strength, lose weight, or improve flexibility. The app adjusts your workouts based on your performance as you progress, ensuring you're constantly challenged but not overwhelmed.

This concept of personalized learning paths extends to other areas as well. If you're learning to code, Codecademy and Treehouse use AI to assess your skills and suggest the proper lessons based on your knowledge and progress. These apps adapt in real time, so you're always learning what's most relevant to you.

AI for Career Development

AI can also be a game-changer in career development, preparing you for the future. If you're looking to gain new skills for a career shift or simply to enhance your current job performance, many AI-powered tools can help. These tools can recommend courses based on your profile, interests, and career goals, helping you find relevant courses to advance your career and boosting your confidence in your professional growth.

Platforms like LinkedIn Learning use AI to recommend courses based on your profile, interests, and career goals. Whether you want to learn about digital marketing, project management, or data analysis, these platforms can help you find relevant courses to advance your career.

AI can also help with resume building and interview preparation. Tools like Jobscan and Resumake use AI to analyze job descriptions and tailor your resume accordingly, ensuring that it's optimized to catch the attention of recruiters. Additionally, AI-driven interview platforms like

HireVue simulates real interview scenarios, helping you practice your responses and gain valuable feedback.

Using AI tools to learn new skills and advance your career, you can position yourself for growth, whether you want to move up in your current role or switch to something completely different.

AI in Online Education

Traditional classrooms are not the only places to learn; online learning has become increasingly popular, and AI plays a huge role in this shift. Many online platforms use AI to create a more interactive, engaging, and personalized learning experience.

Take edX or Udemy, for example. These platforms offer a variety of courses in different fields, but their AI algorithms are what set them apart. These platforms analyze your learning patterns, suggest courses based on your goals, and offer personalized quizzes and activities to reinforce key concepts. The AI can also give you insights into your learning progress, showing you areas where you may need more time.

AI in education also allows for adaptive learning, where the course material adjusts to your understanding. If you master a concept quickly, the material will move on to more advanced topics. If you're struggling with a particular topic, the AI will provide extra resources to help you understand it better.

Using AI for Lifelong Learning

In today's fast-paced world, lifelong learning is more important than ever. AI can help make it easier to continue growing throughout your life. Whether you want to pick up a new hobby, learn a new career skill, or simply stay curious. AI-powered tools and apps make it possible to keep learning at any age.

For example, suppose you've always wanted to learn to play chess. In that case, Chess.com uses AI to offer lessons, tutorials, and even practice games with AI opponents. The app adapts to your skill level, ensuring that you're constantly improving without feeling overwhelmed.

Similarly, apps like Blinkist condense the key ideas from non-fiction books into bite-sized summaries, allowing you to learn new concepts on the go. Whether interested in psychology, business, or self-development, Blinkist gives you the tools to expand your knowledge base.

The best part? You don't have to commit to hours of study. With AI, you can learn at your own pace, fit education into your schedule, and revisit materials as often as you need.

The Future of Learning with AI

Looking ahead, the possibilities for AI in learning are endless. Imagine virtual tutors powered by AI that can help you master any subject or learning platform, predict what skills you'll need in the future, and offer courses to prepare you.

As AI evolves, it will become even better at adapting to your needs, providing personalized learning experiences that help you grow in ways you never thought possible.

AI is not just for scientists or tech experts—it's for everyone. Whether you want to learn a new hobby, acquire career-enhancing skills, or just keep your mind sharp, AI can be your personal learning assistant, helping you reach your goals. With its ability to personalize learning experiences and provide instant feedback. AI makes learning more manageable, efficient, and enjoyable.

In the next chapter, we'll explore how you can use AI to improve your mental and physical well-being, helping you live a healthier, more balanced life.

MENTAL AND PHYSICAL WELL-BEING

In today's fast-paced world, it cannot be easy to maintain a balanced and healthy lifestyle. Between work, family, and other responsibilities, taking care of your mental and physical well-being often gets pushed back. The good news is that AI can be a powerful tool to help you take better care of yourself mentally and physically. This chapter will explore how AI can support your health and wellness journey by providing personalized advice, tracking your progress, and helping you stay motivated. For instance, AI-powered apps like Sleep Cycle and Pillow can be particularly beneficial if you aim to improve your sleep.

AI for Mental Health and Stress Management

Your mental health is just as important as your physical health, and AI has the potential to help you manage stress, anxiety, and even depression. With AI-powered apps and tools, you can access support whenever needed, providing relief and reducing stress without needing in-person appointments.

For example, Woebot is an AI-powered chatbot designed to help users with their mental health. It uses Cognitive Behavioral Therapy (CBT) techniques to help you manage stress, anxiety, and negative thinking. The

Chatbot engages you in conversation, offering tips and strategies for challenging emotions. Since it's available 24/7, you can turn to Woebot whenever you need support, even if you're feeling overwhelmed in the middle of the night.

Another example is Replika, an AI companion that learns from your conversations and helps you explore your feelings. Replika offers a non-judgmental space to talk about your emotions, reducing feelings of loneliness and improving mental well-being. It's not a replacement for a therapist, but it can be a valuable tool for people who want to work through emotions or simply talk to someone when feeling down.

These apps can help you track your mood, identify patterns, and provide helpful coping strategies. While they don't replace professional therapy, they can be an excellent starting point for managing stress and taking care of your mental health.

AI for Sleep Improvement

Good quality sleep is essential for overall well-being, yet many people struggle to get enough rest. AI can help you improve your sleep patterns by offering personalized recommendations and tracking your sleep habits, making you feel cared for and more in control of your well-being.

Apps like Sleep Cycle and Pillow use AI to analyze your sleep patterns and wake you up at the ideal time during your sleep cycle. These apps track your sleep quality, including the time you spend in deep sleep, light sleep, and REM sleep, helping you understand what factors affect your rest.

Some apps even offer personalized sleep tips, such as adjusting the temperature of your room or suggesting relaxation techniques before bedtime. For example, Calm and Headspace offer guided meditations and relaxation exercises that use AI to recommend the best practices based on your current sleep patterns and mood.

By using AI to monitor and improve your sleep, you can wake up feeling refreshed and energized, which in turn helps you maintain better physical and mental health.

AI for Fitness and Physical Health

Regarding physical health, AI can be a game-changer that helps you stay fit and active. Whether you're looking to lose weight, build muscle, or improve your overall fitness, AI-powered fitness apps can guide you through workouts, track your progress, and motivate you to stay on track.

Fitness trackers like Fitbit and Apple Watch are powered by AI that monitors your daily activity, heart rate, steps, calories burned, and even your sleep patterns. These devices provide personalized recommendations to help you achieve your fitness goals, whether taking more steps, increasing your exercise intensity, or improving your sleep quality.

Apps like MyFitnessPal and Lose It! use AI to help you track your diet and exercise. These apps offer personalized meal plans and workouts, adjusting them as you progress. If you're trying to lose weight, the AI will provide insights into your calorie intake and help you stay within your goal range.

For people who enjoy home workouts, apps like Aaptiv and Freeletics offer AI-generated workout routines that adapt to your fitness level and goals. These apps provide real-time feedback, correcting your form and suggesting alternative exercises.

AI for Meditation and Mindfulness

Mindfulness and meditation are powerful practices for improving mental well-being, but getting started can feel intimidating for beginners. AI can help make meditation and mindfulness easier to integrate into your daily routine.

Apps like Headspace and Calm use AI to personalize your meditation sessions based on your goals, whether reducing stress, improving focus, or sleeping better. These apps offer guided meditation sessions of varying lengths, allowing you to choose the right level of guidance based on your needs.

In addition to meditation, these apps often include soundscapes or breathing exercises to help you relax and unwind. By using AI to customize your mindfulness practices, you'll be able to find routines that work best for you, allowing you to improve your focus, reduce anxiety, and promote overall emotional well-being.

AI for Healthy Habits and Routine Building

One of the biggest challenges in maintaining a healthy lifestyle is staying consistent. AI can help you create and stick to healthy habits by providing reminders, tracking your progress, and offering motivation.

Apps like Habitica and Streaks use AI to help you build healthy habits, such as drinking water, exercising regularly, or eating more vegetables. These apps track your daily activities and reward you for consistency, helping you stay motivated even when things get tough.

For example, Noom is an AI-powered app that helps you build healthier eating habits. It uses AI to create personalized meal plans and provide real-time feedback on your eating patterns. Noom's approach is based on psychology, helping you understand the emotional triggers behind unhealthy habits and offering tools to overcome them.

These habit-building apps can help you stay on track with your physical and mental health goals, making developing long-term, sustainable habits easier.

AI for Overall Well-Being

In addition to focusing on specific mental and physical health aspects, AI can help you maintain an overall sense of well-being by offering personalized advice and recommendations across different areas of your life.

For instance, AI-based apps like LifeSum or HealthifyMe track various aspects of your lifestyle, such as diet, exercise, sleep, and mental well-being, and offer personalized suggestions to improve your overall health. These apps help you take a holistic approach to well-being, guiding you to make healthier choices in multiple areas of life.

AI can also improve social well-being by connecting you with others. For example, apps like Meetup use AI to suggest groups or activities based on your interests and location, helping you find new social opportunities and build meaningful connections with others.

AI isn't just a tool for work or productivity—it's also an excellent resource for improving mental and physical well-being. From stress management and sleep improvement to fitness and healthy habits, AI can help you take charge of your health in ways that are personalized, accessible, and effective. By incorporating AI into your wellness routine, you'll have a powerful ally to support your journey to better health.

In the next chapter, we'll explore how AI can help you make smarter financial decisions, save money, and even invest in the future.

MANAGING YOUR FINANCES

Managing money can often feel daunting, especially when there are numerous aspects to consider—budgeting, saving for the future, investing, and even handling debt. However, introducing AI can significantly simplify this process, giving you the tools to make informed financial decisions. This chapter will explore how AI can alleviate the stress of managing your finances, enabling you to make wiser spending choices, save money, and even venture into investing. You don't need to be a financial expert to utilize these modern tools.

AI for Budgeting and Tracking Expenses

One of the initial steps in managing your finances is gaining a clear understanding of where your money is being spent. AI can be a valuable tool in this process, assisting you in tracking your expenses, creating budgets, and identifying areas for potential savings. This level of organization and control can significantly improve your financial management.

Apps like Mint and You Need a Budget (YNAB) use AI to categorize transactions and automatically track expenses in real time. You can easily view your finances by linking these apps to your bank accounts and credit cards. They can also provide insights into your spending habits and alert you if you exceed your budget in any category.

For example, Mint can suggest ways to reduce discretionary spending (like dining out or entertainment) and offer reminders to stay on track with your budget. YNAB goes a step further by helping you assign every dollar a purpose, whether for bills, savings, or spending. These AI tools keep you organized and ensure that you stay on top of your financial goals.

If you want to save money, AI tools can help you identify areas where you're overspending and suggest reducing costs. For instance, Trim is an AI-powered app that analyzes your spending and looks for subscriptions you may have forgotten, like streaming services or gym memberships. Trim can even negotiate lower bills for you, such as your cable or internet subscription, by contacting service providers on your behalf.

AI for Saving Money

Once you've mastered your spending, the next step is to start saving. AI can make saving money easier by automating the process and offering personalized savings tips.

Qapital is an app that uses AI to help you set up automatic savings goals. You can create goals for things like a vacation, emergency fund, or big-ticket item, and the app will transfer small amounts of money into your savings account based on your preferences. The AI learns your habits and adjusts the amount you save over time, helping you build up your savings without thinking about it.

Another app, Chime, is a mobile bank that uses AI to round up your purchases to the nearest dollar and deposit the spare change into a savings account. If you buy a coffee for $3.50, Chime will round it up to $4.00

and put the extra 50 cents into savings. These small amounts add up over time, and you're saving without even noticing.

For those who want to maximize their savings, AI can help you find the best high-interest savings accounts or cashback deals. Apps like Cleo use AI to analyze your spending and suggest ways to save money based on your financial habits. For example, it might tell you that you could save 5% on your grocery bill by shopping at a different store, or it could suggest cashback offers based on your regular purchases.

AI for Investing: Getting Started

Investing can often seem complex and daunting, especially for those new to the concept. However, AI can serve as a guiding hand, helping you make informed decisions, manage your investment portfolio, and even start investing with minimal funds. This guidance can instill confidence and security in your financial future.

Robo-advisors, such as Betterment and Wealthfront, use AI to create personalized investment portfolios based on your risk tolerance, financial goals, and timeline. These platforms automate asset investment, buying, and selling based on your preferences. Robo-advisors are ideal for beginners because they do all the heavy lifting, and you don't need an expert to get started.

For example, suppose you want to invest for retirement. In that case, Betterment will ask you questions about your financial goals and risk tolerance and create a diversified portfolio that aligns with your objectives. It will automatically adjust your portfolio over time to keep it aligned with market changes.

Another option is Acorns, an app that rounds up your everyday purchases and invests in spare change. For example, if you buy a coffee for $3.50,

Acorns will round up the purchase to $4.00 and invest 50 cents. This process allows you to invest small amounts of money consistently, making it easy for beginners to start investing.

AI for Credit Scores and Loans

Your credit score is crucial in your financial life, affecting everything from loan approval to interest rates. AI can help you keep track of your credit score and even improve it by offering personalized advice on boosting your credit.

Apps like Credit Karma and Experian use AI to give you an up-to-date view of your credit score and suggest ways to improve it. They analyze your financial behavior and provide insights into how your actions—such as paying off debt or reducing credit card balances—affect your credit score. They can also alert you to changes in your credit report, helping you stay on top of potential issues that could hurt your score.

AI can also help you find the best loan options by analyzing your credit history and comparing rates from different lenders. For example, LendingTree uses AI to match you with loan offers that suit your needs, whether you're looking for a personal loan, mortgage, or auto loan. The app considers your financial situation and recommends the most affordable options, helping you save money on interest and fees.

AI for Retirement Planning

Planning for retirement can seem daunting, but AI can make it easier by helping you create a personalized retirement plan and track your progress toward your goals.

Fidelity's AI-powered tools can help you estimate how much money you'll need for retirement, factoring in your desired lifestyle, current savings, and expected future expenses. It can then recommend investment strategies and savings goals based on your needs.

Another example is Ellevest, an AI-powered platform for women's retirement planning. It considers career breaks, gender pay gaps, and other unique financial challenges to provide personalized advice and investment options that support long-term retirement goals.

AI can help you stay on track with your retirement goals by automating contributions to your retirement accounts and offering personalized investment advice. The key is to start early, and AI can make it easier to get there.

Managing your finances doesn't have to be complicated. With the help of AI-powered tools and apps, you can track your spending, save money, invest for the future, and even improve your credit score—all with minimal effort. These tools can help you make smarter financial decisions, no matter where you are in your financial journey.

In the next chapter, we'll explore how AI can help you improve your productivity, streamline your daily tasks, and simplify your life by automating some of your everyday responsibilities.

THINGS I NEED TO REVIEW AGAIN

_____

_____

_____

_____

_____

_____

_____

_____

THINGS I WANT TO REMEMBER

_____

_____

_____

_____

_____

_____

_____

_____

AUTOMATING TASKS

In the hustle and bustle of our busy lives, it's all too common to feel overwhelmed with everything we have to do. From keeping track of our schedules to replying to messages and managing personal projects, it often feels like there's just not enough time in the day. But imagine if artificial intelligence could come to the rescue and help us make the most of our time by caring for those everyday tasks. In this section, we're thrilled to explore how AI can be your productivity buddy—helping you streamline your routines, organize your to-do lists, and give you back the time to focus on what matters to you.

AI for Managing Your Schedule and Calendar

AI's most significant time-saving benefit is its ability to manage your calendar and appointments. It provides a welcome relief from the stress of back-and-forth emails, time zone confusion, and missed meetings, allowing you to focus on more critical tasks.

Apps like Google Calendar and Microsoft Outlook use AI to help you organize your schedule more efficiently. These tools can automatically detect conflicting events and suggest the best time for new appointments.

They can also send reminders, helping you stay on top of your commitments without thinking about it.

Another powerful tool is Clara, an AI-powered scheduling assistant that takes over finding a time for meetings. You simply email Clara your meeting request, and the AI will find a time that works for you and the other participants, eliminating the need for endless email exchanges.

For those with busy work schedules, **x.ai** offers an AI-powered personal assistant that can schedule meetings, send reminders, and even reschedule if necessary. The AI communicates directly with your contacts and works on your behalf, saving you time and reducing the mental load of managing your calendar.

AI for Organizing Your Tasks and To-Do Lists

Managing a long list of tasks can feel overwhelming, but AI can help you take control. It can help you prioritize tasks, break them down into manageable steps, and keep you on track, making the process more manageable and less daunting.

Apps like Todoist and Trello use AI to help you organize your to-do lists and projects. Todoist, for example, offers innovative scheduling features that allow you to prioritize tasks based on urgency and deadlines. It can even learn from your behavior, suggesting when to schedule tasks based on when you typically have time to work on them.

Trello is a visual task management app that uses AI to organize your tasks into boards, lists, and cards. The AI helps you stay on track by recommending which tasks to focus on next. It can also integrate with other productivity tools like Slack and Google Drive, creating a streamlined workflow to help you easily manage multiple projects.

ClickUp combines AI with project management, task tracking, and time management features if you want a more automated approach. It can help you break larger projects into smaller tasks, assign priorities, and set deadlines. It also allows you to automate repetitive tasks, like creating new cards for recurring activities or automatically moving functions to the next step.

AI for Email Management and Communication

Email can be a huge time sink, but AI can help you manage your emails more efficiently and less time-consumingly. It can filter out spam, sort messages, and even respond to certain emails automatically, giving you more time to focus on essential tasks.

For instance, SaneBox is an AI-powered tool that helps you manage your inbox by sorting messages into folders based on importance. It automatically filters out unimportant emails so you can focus on the ones that matter most. SaneBox can also set up reminders for follow-up emails and even clean out old, irrelevant messages, helping you maintain a clutter-free inbox.

Find yourself typing similar responses repeatedly. AI tools like Boomerang and Respondable can help you write better emails faster. Boomerang uses AI to suggest improvements to your email drafts, helping you make your messages more transparent and effective. It can also schedule emails to be sent at the perfect time, ensuring that your message arrives when it's most likely to be read.

Grammarly is another useful AI tool that helps you improve your writing by offering suggestions for grammar, tone, and clarity. Whether you're writing an email, a report, or a social media post, Grammarly can ensure your message is professional and easy to understand.

AI for Time Management and Focus

Staying focused and managing your time effectively can be difficult, especially with so many distractions competing for your attention. AI-powered tools can help you stay on task and maximize your time.

For example, Focus@Will is an AI-powered music service designed to help you concentrate. It offers personalized playlists based on your work style and the task you're working on. Whether you are writing, brainstorming, or doing deep work, Focus@Will uses AI to select the best music to boost productivity and reduce distractions.

RescueTime is another helpful tool that tracks your time on your devices and offers insights into where you're losing focus. It can help you identify time-wasting habits and recommend ways to stay on task. The AI can block distracting websites during designated work periods, helping you maintain focus.

If you struggle with procrastination, AI tools like Beeminder can help you stay accountable to your goals. Beeminder uses AI to track your progress toward specific goals and sends reminders when you're falling behind. It even includes a financial incentive—if you don't meet your goals, you'll have to pay a penalty. This can help you stay motivated and on track to complete tasks on time.

AI for Automating Repetitive Tasks

Many everyday tasks can take a lot of time, from managing social media accounts to creating reports. AI can help you automate these repetitive tasks, freeing up more time for the work that requires your attention and creativity.

For example, Zapier is an AI-powered tool that connects different apps and automates workflows. You can set up "Zaps" to perform tasks automatically, such as posting updates to your social media accounts or creating new functions in your project management tool when you receive a specific email. This kind of automation can save you hours of manual work each week.

If you use spreadsheets often, Google Sheets has built-in AI features that help automate data entry, perform complex calculations, and even generate reports. For instance, you can set up AI to automatically categorize and analyze data, making extracting valuable insights from your spreadsheets easier without doing all the work yourself.

AI tools like IFTTT (If This Then That) allow you to automate actions across multiple apps. For instance, you can set up an automation where every time you receive an email with an attachment, it's automatically saved to your cloud storage. This reduces the need for manual file management and ensures that nothing slips through the cracks.

AI isn't just for big businesses or tech experts—it can be a valuable tool for anyone looking to boost their productivity and streamline their daily tasks. From managing your schedule and to-do lists to automating repetitive tasks and staying focused, AI can help you save time, stay organized, and get more done. By incorporating AI into your routine, you can reclaim time for the things that truly matter, whether focusing on your work, spending time with family, or simply relaxing and unwinding.

TOPICS THAT HAVE INSPIRED ME

AI: ART, MUSIC, AND WRITING

When people think of AI, they often imagine it solving problems, processing data, or automating tasks. However, AI is also a catalyst for transformation in the creative world, inspiring us with its potential to generate new ideas and stimulate our artistic senses. It's now used to paint pictures, compose music, and even write novels, sparking a new wave of creativity.

But can AI be creative? Can a machine make art or write a song like a human? The short answer is not exactly—but it can be a powerful tool to support and enhance human creativity. AI doesn't have feelings, personal experiences, or a deep understanding of culture. Still, it can analyze patterns, mimic styles, and generate new content that artists, musicians, and writers can refine and enhance, reaffirming the unique value of human creativity.

In this chapter, we'll explore how AI is used in art, music, and writing, highlighting the best AI tools that are not just for experts but also for beginners who are eager to unleash their creative potential. We'll also delve into the future of AI-driven creativity, inspiring you to be part of this exciting future.

AI in Art: Can a Machine Be an Artist?

Imagine typing a few words—like *"a futuristic city at sunset"*—and watching AI generate a stunning digital painting in seconds. This is the magic of AI-generated art, where computers create unique images based on text descriptions.

AI-powered tools like DALL·E, Deep Dream, and Runway ML use machine learning to study millions of artworks. They learn how different styles, colors, and patterns work together, allowing them to generate entirely new pieces of art based on what they've learned.

How AI-Generated Art Works

AI art tools use a special type of AI called generative AI, which learns from massive collections of paintings, drawings, and photographs. When you give the AI a text prompt like "a cat wearing sunglasses in a cyberpunk city," it doesn't just copy existing art—it creates something entirely new based on patterns it has learned.

Popular AI Art Tools

- DALL·E (OpenAI) – It generates original images from text descriptions.

- Deep Dream Generator (Google) – Transforms images into dream-like art.

- Runway ML (Runway) – AI-powered video and image editing for artists.

- Canva AI (Canva) – helps non-artists create graphics and designs.

AI vs. Human Artists: What's the Difference?

While AI can generate stunning images, it lacks human emotion, intent, and originality. Human artists create with purpose, expressing thoughts, feelings, and cultural meanings that AI simply doesn't understand. Many artists see AI as a tool to enhance their work rather than a replacement.

For example, artists may use AI to:

- Brainstorm ideas and experiment with different styles.

- Automate repetitive tasks, like resizing and color correction.

- Enhance traditional artwork by adding AI-generated elements.

AI in Music: Composing the Soundtrack of the Future

AI is also changing the music world, allowing people to compose entire songs without playing an instrument or understanding music theory.

AI-powered music tools can:

- Compose new melodies and harmonies.

- Suggest lyrics based on mood or theme.

- Remix existing songs into new versions.

How AI Creates Music

AI music generators like AIVA, Boomy, and Magenta work by analyzing thousands of pieces of music across different genres. The AI learns patterns in melodies, rhythms, and chord progressions and then generates new music based on what it has learned.

For example, you can tell an AI tool:

- "Create a relaxing jazz song"

- "Generate an upbeat pop melody"

- "Compose a soundtrack for a sci-fi movie."

The AI will then build a song from scratch with instruments and harmonies!

Popular AI Music Tools

- AIVA (aiva.ai) – Composes classical and modern music.

- Boomy (boomy.com) – An AI-powered tool for beginners to make songs.

- Magenta (Google) – AI experiments in music composition.

- Amper Music (Amper) – AI-generated soundtracks for content creators.

Can AI Replace Human Musicians?

Not really! AI can generate music but lacks the emotional depth and storytelling ability that human composers bring to their work. Many musicians use AI as a co-writer, helping to create ideas or speed up the creative process.

For example, artists can:

- Use AI to generate song structures, then refine them with their creativity.

- Remix AI-generated loops and beats into original compositions.

- Use AI for sound design in movies and video games.

AI won't replace human musicians but will expand creative possibilities, making music composition more accessible.

AI in Writing: Can AI Write Like a Human?

AI isn't just making music and images and writing books, poems, and news articles. AI writing tools have become so advanced that they can generate entire blog posts, scripts, and even novels!

How AI Generates Text

AI writing tools like ChatGPT, Jasper AI, and Sudowrite are trained on millions of books, articles, and conversations. When you give AI a prompt, it predicts what words should come next based on patterns in human language.

For example, you could ask AI to:

- "Write a short story about a time-traveling scientist."

- "Create a marketing email for a new coffee shop."

- "Generate a poem about the changing seasons."

The AI will instantly create coherent, human-like text based on your request.

Popular AI Writing Tools

- ChatGPT (OpenAI) – An AI-powered chatbot for writing and brainstorming.

- Jasper AI (jasper.ai) – AI for marketing copy and content creation.

- Grammarly AI (grammarly.com) – An AI-powered grammar and style assistant.

- Sudowrite (sudowrite.com) – An AI tool for creative writers and novelists.

AI vs. Human Writers: Can AI Write Better?

While AI can generate text quickly, it lacks human creativity, emotion, and personal experiences. AI doesn't understand humor, culture, or deep storytelling as humans do.

Many writers use AI to:

- Overcome writer's block by generating ideas.

- Improve their writing with AI-powered editing.

- Speed up the process of drafting blog posts and articles.

AI is a helpful assistant, but it can't replace the depth of human storytelling.

Final Thoughts: AI as a Creative Tool

So, can AI be creative? Not in the same way humans are, but it can be a potent tool to assist creativity. AI allows anyone, even beginners, to create music, write stories, and make digital art without formal training.

AI won't replace artists, musicians, or writers—it will empower them. AI makes it easier if you've ever wanted to explore your creative side. Whether designing graphics, composing music, or writing stories, AI can help you bring your ideas to life faster and more efficiently.

Amanda Fleish

NOTES AND IDEAS

CYBERSECURITY IN THE DIGITAL AGE

Imagine waking up one morning to find that someone has hacked into your email, stolen your personal information, and even gained access to your bank account. Scary, right? Unfortunately, cybercrime is becoming more sophisticated. AI is now playing a role on both sides—helping hackers break into systems and protecting people from cyber threats.

But don't worry—AI is one of the strongest defenses against cyberattacks. In this chapter, we'll explore how AI, a technology that can learn and make decisions like humans, is used to enhance security, how cybercriminals also use AI to their advantage, and, most importantly, what you can do to protect yourself in the digital world.

How AI Helps Keep You Safe Online

Cybersecurity has always been about staying one step ahead of hackers. AI has given security experts a powerful new tool to do just that. AI

It doesn't just react to threats; it proactively scans millions of threats in real time, detects unusual activity, and even predicts potential cyberattacks before they happen, providing a strong sense of security.

AI Detects Suspicious Activity Faster Than Humans

AI-powered cybersecurity tools can instantly analyze vast amounts of data and spot security threats.

- Have you ever received a fraud alert from your bank about a suspicious transaction? That's AI at work!

- Companies like Google and Microsoft use AI to scan billions of emails daily to block phishing scams.

- AI helps websites and businesses detect hacking attempts by spotting unusual login patterns.

AI Helps Identify and Block Phishing Scams

Phishing is when hackers trick you into giving them personal information, like passwords or credit card numbers. You've probably seen emails that say:

Your account has been compromised! Click this link to verify your identity."

Most phishing scams look real, but AI can analyze email patterns and detect fake messages before they reach your inbox. Tools like Google Safe Browsing and Microsoft Defender use AI to flag fraudulent websites and warn you before accidentally entering your password on a fake login page.

AI Strengthens Password Security

Did you know that 123456 is still one of the most commonly used passwords? (Yes, really!) AI can help create and manage strong passwords so you don't have to remember them all.

AI-powered password managers:

Password (1password.com)

LastPass (lastpass.com)

AI can generate super-strong passwords and autofill them securely when you log into websites. That way, you're not using the same weak password everywhere, making it harder for hackers to break into your accounts.

How Hackers Are Using AI for Cybercrime

Unfortunately, hackers are also using AI—but for the wrong reasons. Cybercriminals have found ways to train AI to break security systems, making cyberattacks more advanced.

Hackers use AI to guess passwords by testing thousands of combinations per second. If someone uses a weak password, AI-powered hacking tools can break it in minutes.

This is why security experts recommend two-factor authentication (2FA)—which we'll discuss later—to add an extra layer of security to your accounts.

Deepfake Scams:

You may have seen deepfake videos, where AI creates fake images or voice recordings of real people. Some deepfake scams are harmless fun, but others are used to impersonate real people, like your boss or a family member, tricking victims into revealing sensitive information.

For example, cybercriminals have used deepfake voice cloning to impersonate company CEOs, tricking employees into wiring millions of dollars to fake accounts. As AI improves at mimicking human voices and faces, deepfake scams will become even more challenging to detect.

AI-Powered Phishing Attacks

Cybercriminals now use AI-generated phishing emails that look even more convincing than before.

- Old phishing emails had terrible grammar and spelling mistakes, making them easy to spot.

- AI-generated phishing emails sound professional and honest, making it harder to tell what's fake.

This is why AI-powered security tools are more critical than ever.

Protect Yourself from AI-Driven Cybercrime

Now that you know the pros and cons of AI in cybersecurity, let's discuss how to stay safe.

Use Strong, AI-Generated Passwords

Instead of using weak passwords like "password123", use a password manager to generate and store complex passwords that hackers can't easily guess.

Tip: Never reuse passwords for multiple accounts!

Turn on Two-Factor Authentication (2FA)

2FA adds an extra security step before logging into your account—like sending a verification code to your phone.

Tip: Always enable 2FA on essential accounts, like banking and email accounts.

Be Wary of AI-Generated Emails and Deepfake Videos

If an email looks suspicious, even if it appears to be from someone you trust, don't click on links or open attachments until you verify that it's real.

Tip: If in doubt, contact the person directly instead of replying to the email.

Keep Your Software and Devices Updated

AI-powered security software, such as Windows Defender, Mac Security, and antivirus apps, helps keep your system protected from new threats.

Tip: Always install security updates on your phone and computer!

Avoid Public Wi-Fi Without a VPN

Hackers love public Wi-Fi (like in coffee shops and airports) because they can steal personal information from unsecured networks.

Tip: If you must use public Wi-Fi, use a VPN (Virtual Private Network) to encrypt your data.

Use AI-Powered Security Tools

Here are some beginner-friendly security tools that use AI to keep you safe:

- Bitdefender AI (bitdefender.com) – AI-powered antivirus and malware protection.

- Norton 360 AI (norton.com) – AI-driven cybersecurity for personal devices.

- Malwarebytes (malwarebytes.com) – AI-based malware detection.

The Future of AI and Cybersecurity

As AI advances, so will both cybercrime and security measures. The good news is that AI-driven security tools will continue to get smarter at detecting threats before they happen. In the future, we can expect:

- AI-powered voice authentication instead of passwords.

- Smarter fraud detection for online banking.

- AI automatically blocks deepfake scams before they spread.

Cybersecurity constantly evolves, and staying informed is the best way to protect yourself.

Final Thoughts: Stay Safe, Stay Smart

AI is a powerful security tool and a weapon for hackers, but you can avoid cyber threats by taking a few wise precautions.

Remember:

- Use strong passwords and 2FA

- Be cautious of AI-powered phishing emails

- Keep your devices and security software updated.

- Avoid public Wi-Fi without a VPN

The digital world is exciting, but staying aware and safe is essential. With AI on our side, the future of cybersecurity is looking brighter than ever!

THINGS I STILL DON'T UNDERSTAND

_____

_____

_____

_____

_____

_____

_____

_____

_____

THINGS THAT HAVE MOTIVATED ME

_____

_____

_____

_____

_____

_____

_____

_____

AI FOR SOCIAL GOOD

When most people hear "artificial intelligence," they often think about robots, automation, and big tech companies. But AI is doing far more than just making our lives more convenient—it's helping solve some of the world's biggest challenges.

From fighting climate change to advancing medical research, AI is used for social good, improving lives in ways we may not always see. This chapter will explore how AI positively impacts healthcare, environmental conservation, accessibility, education, and disaster response.

AI in Healthcare

AI's most promising application is in healthcare, where it is transforming how we diagnose diseases, develop treatments, and predict health risks. This transformative power of AI in healthcare is a beacon of hope, promising a future where diseases can be detected and treated more effectively than ever before.

Detecting Diseases Earlier and More Accurately

Imagine a world where cancer can be detected months or even years earlier—that's exactly what AI is helping doctors do. AI-powered medical imaging tools analyze X-rays, MRIs, and CT scans with incredible accuracy, sometimes detecting early signs of diseases like cancer, tuberculosis, and strokes that even highly trained doctors might miss.

Example: Google's AI system for breast cancer detection outperformed human radiologists in identifying tumors in mammograms, catching cancerous growths that were previously overlooked.

Predicting Disease Outbreaks

AI can track and predict the spread of diseases, helping governments and healthcare organizations prepare for outbreaks before they happen.

Example: During the COVID-19 pandemic, an AI program called BlueDot predicted the virus outbreak before official reports by analyzing news articles, flight data, and government reports in different languages.

AI in Drug Discovery

Developing new medicines usually takes years, but AI can analyze massive amounts of data and identify potential drug candidates much faster.

Example: AI helped researchers at DeepMind predict the structure of proteins, solving a 50-year-old scientific puzzle and paving the way for faster drug development for diseases like Alzheimer's and Parkinson's.

AI in Environmental Conservation

AI is also used to fight climate change, protect endangered species, and reduce pollution.

Fighting Climate Change

AI helps scientists analyze weather patterns, carbon emissions, and deforestation rates to find better solutions for protecting our planet.

Example: AI-powered climate models help predict extreme weather events like hurricanes and wildfires, allowing communities to prepare before disaster strikes.

Protecting Endangered Animals

AI is used to track and protect endangered species, helping conservationists prevent illegal hunting and habitat destruction.

Example: AI-powered cameras and drones monitor elephants, tigers, and rhinos in Africa and Asia, alerting park rangers when poachers are nearby.

Google's AI system analyzes whale songs to track populations and understand their migration patterns, helping marine biologists protect them from ship collisions and Pollution.

Reducing Pollution

AI is helping cities become more energy-efficient by analyzing traffic, electricity use, and air pollution data.

Example: AI-powered traffic lights in cities like Pittsburgh, USA, adjust in real time to reduce traffic jams, lowering fuel consumption and air pollution.

AI for Accessibility: Helping People with Disabilities

AI is making technology more accessible for people with disabilities, breaking down barriers, and improving independence.

AI-Powered Speech and Text Tools

For individuals who are deaf or hard of hearing, AI can convert speech into text in real time, making conversations and videos more accessible.

Example: Apps like Google Live Transcribe and Otter.ai provide instant captions for conversations, helping the deaf and hard-of-hearing community communicate more easily.

AI for the Visually Impaired

For those who are blind or have low vision, AI can describe their surroundings, read text aloud, and even recognize faces.

Example: Microsoft's Seeing AI app uses AI to read signs, scan barcodes, and identify objects using a smartphone camera.

Smart Assistants for Mobility

AI-powered voice assistants like Amazon Alexa, Google Assistant, and Siri help people with limited mobility control their devices, from turning on lights to setting reminders using their voice.

Non-Techi Guide to Artificial Intelligence

AI in Education: Personalized Learning

In education, AI is transforming learning and enhancing its engagement and effectiveness for students around the globe. By offering tailored learning experiences that address unique strengths and weaknesses, AI ignites a fresh wave of curiosity and excitement in the educational process.

Personalized Learning

Not all students learn the same way or at the same pace. AI-powered learning platforms analyze students' progress and provide customized lessons to help them learn better.

Example: Apps like Khan Academy AI and Duolingo adjust lesson difficulty based on a student's strengths and weaknesses, making learning more engaging and effective.

AI Tutoring and Homework Help

AI-powered tutoring apps help students understand complex subjects by explaining concepts step by step.

Example: AI tutors like Socratic by Google and Photomath allow students to take pictures of their homework questions and get AI-powered explanations.

Bridging the Education Gap

AI is helping students in remote and underdeveloped areas access quality education, even if they don't have teachers nearby.

Example: AI-powered chatbots provide free, 24/7 tutoring to students in low-income countries, giving them access to previously unavailable knowledge.

AI in Disaster Response and Humanitarian Efforts

AI is also helping during natural disasters, humanitarian crises, and emergencies, speeding up rescue efforts and making them more efficient.

Predicting and Responding to Natural Disasters

AI can analyze satellite images and weather patterns to predict earthquakes, floods, and wildfires before they happen.

For example, AI models at NASA and IBM can forecast hurricanes and floods days in advance, allowing governments to evacuate at-risk areas.

AI-Powered Emergency Response

During disasters, AI-powered chatbots and apps help victims find shelters, food, and emergency services in real-time.

Example: The Google Crisis Response Team uses AI to provide real-time disaster alerts and evacuation maps during hurricanes and earthquakes.

AI for Refugee and Crisis Aid

AI is used to help refugees and displaced communities by providing translation tools and emergency assistance.

Example: The UN's AI-powered translation tool helps refugees communicate in different languages, making it easier to access help and resources.

AI as a Force for Good

AI isn't just about technology and business—it's changing the world for the better. From saving lives and protecting nature to helping people with disabilities and providing education, AI impacts us in ways we never imagined.

The best part? These advancements are just the beginning. AI will bring even more life-changing innovations, helping people in ways we can't predict. By understanding and embracing AI, we can be part of a future where technology is used for social good, not just convenience.

Amanda Fleish

NOTES

THE FUTURE OF AI: WHAT'S NEXT?

As explored in this book, AI has already made its way into many aspects of our lives, from managing our finances to staying productive and organized. But we've only scratched the surface. The future of AI holds exciting possibilities, and it's poised to impact even more areas of our lives in ways we can't fully imagine yet. In this final chapter, we'll look at what the future of AI might hold, how it will continue to evolve, and what it means for you—whether you're a beginner or someone already using AI tools in your daily routine.

The Rise of AI in Everyday Life

AI will become an even more integral part of our daily lives as technology advances. We use AI for voice assistants, smart home devices, and financial apps. Still, these technologies will soon become even more powerful and intuitive. Consider how voice assistants like Siri or Alexa can recognize natural language and respond to commands. In the future, these AI assistants can anticipate your needs before you even ask.

Envision an AI that understands your preferences so well that it can handle tasks like adjusting the thermostat, ordering groceries, or managing your calendar without you having to lift a finger. This level of convenience will allow you to concentrate more on meaningful tasks and less on repetitive, everyday chores, relieving you of unnecessary burdens.

Beyond the home, AI will continue transforming healthcare, education, and business. AI will analyze medical data, predict health outcomes, and help doctors diagnose more accurately. In education, AI-powered tutoring systems will personalize lessons for each student, helping them learn at their own pace and best. AI will automate even more complex tasks in the business world, enabling companies to innovate faster and provide better customer service.

The Evolution of AI: Smarter, More Personalized Tools

One of AI's most exciting qualities is its ability to learn and adapt. As AI evolves, it will become even more personalized, offering solutions tailored to your unique needs and preferences.

Right now, AI tools are helpful but often require us to provide input and data. In the future, AI can anticipate our needs without explicit instructions. For example, AI might learn your daily routine—when you wake up, exercise, or work—and suggest ways to improve your productivity or health, offering helpful nudges based on your habits.

Imagine a personal assistant who not only schedules your meetings but also suggests the best times for you to take breaks, recommends healthy meal options, or even adjusts your environment based on your mood. AI will help create a more seamless and personalized experience in all aspects of life.

The next evolution of AI will also include improved natural language processing (NLP), allowing AI to understand better and respond to human speech. This means that voice assistants and chatbots will become more fluent, hold meaningful conversations with you, and provide deeper insights and suggestions.

How Automation Will Change Our Work

Many people are concerned about how AI will impact jobs. Automation is already replacing specific manufacturing, customer service, and healthcare tasks. However, rather than eliminating jobs, AI will likely change the nature of work, creating new opportunities and demands for different skill sets.

For instance, while AI may handle some routine administrative tasks, it will also create new roles that require human creativity, emotional intelligence, and decision-making. People skilled at working with AI tools will be in high demand as businesses look for individuals who can effectively manage and collaborate with AI systems.

For example, AI trainers, who teach AI algorithms how to learn and improve, and AI ethics specialists, who help ensure that AI is used responsibly and moderately, are just two of the many roles emerging as AI becomes more integrated into different industries.

Furthermore, the rise of AI-driven entrepreneurship will create new opportunities for individuals to build businesses around AI-powered tools, applications, and services. As AI becomes more accessible, anyone can develop their products or services, offering innovative solutions to real-world problems.

Ethical Considerations: Ensuring AI Benefits Everyone

As AI continues to evolve, we must also consider the ethical implications of these technologies. Privacy, bias, and accountability will become increasingly important as AI integrates into our lives.

For example, as AI tools collect more personal data to offer personalized recommendations and services, it's essential to ensure that this data is protected and used responsibly. AI systems must be transparent, meaning users should understand how their data is collected and used. Striking the right balance between personalization and privacy will be critical.

Additionally, AI must be designed to be fair and unbiased. If AI algorithms are trained on data that reflects past inequalities, they can sometimes unintentionally perpetuate bias. Developing inclusive, equitable, and bias-free algorithms ensures that AI benefits everyone.

Ethical considerations around AI will require collaboration between governments, businesses, and individuals to create laws and policies that promote responsible AI use. By working together, we can help ensure that AI remains a tool that enhances human potential and enriches society, making you feel included and part of a responsible community.

Preparing for an AI-Driven Future

The future of AI is bright, but it also requires us to think carefully about how we use these powerful technologies. It's essential to stay informed, adapt to new changes, and continue learning to maximize what AI offers. Whether you're just starting to explore AI or are already using it in your daily life, the key to success is to embrace these changes and see them as opportunities for growth.

Here are a few things you can do to prepare for an AI-driven future:

- Stay curious: Continue exploring new AI tools and learning how they work. The more you understand, the better equipped you'll be to take advantage of them.

- Adapt and be flexible: As AI evolves, so will the tools and services you use. Stay open to new ways of doing things and embrace change.

- Develop new skills: While AI will automate many tasks, human creativity, emotional intelligence, and critical thinking will always be needed. Consider learning new skills that complement AI technologies, such as coding, data analysis, or digital marketing.

- Ethical awareness: Be mindful of the ethical considerations around AI and support initiatives that prioritize fairness, transparency, and privacy.

Embracing the Power of AI

AI is no longer a futuristic concept—it's here and changing how we live, work, and interact with the world. While there are still challenges to address, the future of AI holds exciting possibilities that can enhance our lives in countless ways. By embracing AI, staying informed, and adapting to the changes it brings, we can unlock its full potential and use it to create a better, more efficient, and more connected world.

And remember: as you now know, you are no longer "technologically impaired" when it comes to AI. You've taken the first steps to understanding these tools. With each new piece of knowledge, you gain more confidence in navigating the AI-powered world.

CONCLUSION: NO LONGER A BEGINNER

AI is Now in Your Toolbox

When you first picked up this book, you might have felt that artificial intelligence was complicated, intimidating, or reserved for tech experts. But now, you know the truth—AI is not just for programmers and scientists. It's for you, too.

Throughout this book, we've broken down AI into simple, understandable pieces—without jargon or technical confusion.

You've learned:

What AI is and how it works—from machine learning to neural networks, in a way that makes sense.

How AI already plays a role in your everyday life—whether in your smartphone, email, shopping, or entertainment.

The different types of AI—and why AI assistants, automation tools, and deep learning models all serve various purposes.

How AI is transforming workplaces and productivity—and how you can use it to boost efficiency.

How AI can be your personal assistant—helping you learn, stay organized, and even improve your mental and physical well-being.

 How AI can help you manage finances, automate tasks, and plan your future, saving time and reducing stress.

 The future of AI—where AI is heading and how it will continue shaping our world.

 How AI is being used for social good—improving healthcare, protecting the environment, making education accessible, and even helping in disaster response.

Most importantly, you've shifted from an outsider to an AI user. You now know that AI isn't something to fear—it's a tool. Just like learning to drive a car or use a smartphone, understanding AI is about using it to make life easier, more efficient, and even more fun.

Where Do You Go From Here?

Now that you have a solid foundation, you can:

Continue learning—follow AI news, take short courses, and experiment with AI in small ways.

Use AI wisely. Stay informed about privacy, security, and ethical concerns when using AI safely and responsibly.

Help others understand AI—now that you know the basics, you can explain AI to friends and family, helping them see how it benefits everyday life.

Final Thoughts:

Artificial intelligence is no longer science fiction—it's woven into the fabric of daily life. The best part? You don't need to be a tech expert to use it. AI is here to help; you can make the most of it.

Amanda Fleish

APPENDIX A

AI TOOLS AND RESOURCES

Below is a categorized list of AI-powered apps and tools discussed in this book, their official websites, and how to find them. Many of these tools offer free versions or trials, making it easy for beginners to explore AI without commitment.

AI Chatbots & Virtual Assistants

- ChatGPT – Conversational AI for answering questions, generating content, and brainstorming ideas.
    - Website: https://openai.com/chatgpt
    - Available on: Web, iOS, Android
- Google Bard (Gemini AI) – Google's AI assistant for research, creativity, and productivity.
    - Website: https://bard.google.com
    - Available on: Web
- Microsoft Copilot – An AI-powered assistant integrated with Microsoft apps like Word and Excel.
    - Website: https://www.microsoft.com/en-us/copilot
    - Available on: Web, Windows, Office 365

AI for Writing & Content Creation

- Grammarly – An AI-powered writing assistant for grammar, spelling, and style suggestions.
  - Website: https://www.grammarly.com
  - Available on: Web, Chrome extension, Microsoft Word, Desktop App
- Jasper AI – An AI-powered copywriting tool for marketing, social media, and blog content.
  - Website: https://www.jasper.ai
  - Available on: Web

AI for Image Generation & Editing

- Canva AI (Magic Design) – An AI-powered graphic design and image creation tool.
  - Website: https://www.canva.com
  - Available on: Web, iOS, Android
- DALL·E – An AI image generator for creating unique visuals from text descriptions.
  - Website: https://openai.com/dall-e
  - Available on: Web

- Remove.bg – An AI tool for automatically removing image backgrounds.
  - Website: https://www.remove.bg
  - Available on: Web

AI for Productivity & Organization

- Notion AI – AI-powered notes, task management, and knowledge organization.
  - Website: https://www.notion.so
  - Available on: Web, iOS, Android
- Otter.ai – An AI-powered transcription tool for meetings and interviews.
  - Website: https://otter.ai
  - Available on: Web, iOS, Android

AI for Audio & Video

- Descript – an AI-powered video editing, podcasting, and transcription tool.
  - Website: https://www.descript.com
  - Available on: Web, Desktop App
- ElevenLabs – An AI text-to-speech tool for natural-sounding voice generation.
  - Website: https://elevenlabs.io

o   Available on: Web

AI for Learning & Research

- Elicit – An AI-powered research assistant that helps summarize academic papers.
  - o   Website: https://elicit.org
  - o   Available on: Web
- Perplexity AI – An AI-powered search engine for more in-depth answers than traditional Google searches.
  - o   Website: https://www.perplexity.ai
  - o   Available on: Web, iOz

How to Find These Apps

- Website Access: Use the links provided above.
- App Stores: Many apps can be found on the Apple App Store or Google Play Store by searching their names.
- Browser Extensions: Some AI tools (like Grammarly and
- ChatGPT) offer Chrome extensions for quick access.

APPENDIX B

FINANCIAL APPS SUMMARY

Budgeting & Saving Apps

- Acorns – Rounds up everyday purchases and invests the spare change.
  - Website: https://www.acorns.com
- Chime – A Mobile banking app with automated savings features.
  - Website: https://www.chime.com
- Cleo – An AI-powered budgeting app providing spending insights and savings suggestions.
  - Website: https://www.meetcleo.com
- Mint Tracks expenses, categorizes transactions, and provides spending insights.
  - Website: https://www.mint.com
- Qapital – Helps users set savings goals and automate transfers.
  - Website: https://www.qapital.com
- YNAB (You Need a Budget) – A Budgeting tool that assigns every dollar a purpose.
  - Website: https://www.ynab.com

Investment & Credit Management Apps

- Betterment – Robo-advisor that creates personalized investment portfolios.
    o Website: https://www.betterment.com
- Credit Karma – Provides free credit scores and financial recommendations.
    o Website: https://www.creditkarma.com
- Experian – Offers credit reports, monitoring, and alerts.
    o Website: https://www.experian.com
- Ellevest – An Investment platform tailored for women.
    o Website: https://www.ellevest.com
- Fidelity – A Financial services provider with investment and retirement options.
    o Website: https://www.fidelity.com
- LendingTree – Compares loan rates from multiple lenders.
    o Website: https://www.lendingtree.com
- Trim – Analyzes spending, cancels unused subscriptions, and negotiates bills.
    o Website: https://www.asktrim.com
- Wealthfront – Robo-advisor for automated investing and financial planning.
    o Website: https://www.wealthfront.com

APPENDIX C

APPS, TOOLS, AND ONLINE COURSES

Adobe Lightroom. (n.d.). *Photo editing and organization software.* https://www.adobe.com/products/photoshop-lightroom.html

Boomerang. (n.d.). *Gmail tool for scheduling and reminders.* https://www.boomeranggmail.com/

Clara. (n.d.). *AI-powered scheduling assistant.* https://claralabs.com/

ClickUp. (n.d.). *Project management and task tracking tool.* https://clickup.com/

Duolingo. (n.d.). *Learn a language for free.* https://www.duolingo.com

Focus@Will. (n.d.). An *AI-powered music service for productivity.* https://www.focusatwill.com/

Freeletics. (n.d.). *Fitness coach & workout app.* https://www.freeletics.com

Grammarly. (n.d.). *AI writing assistant.* https://www.grammarly.com/

HireVue. (n.d.). *AI-driven interview practice platform.* https://www.hirevue.com

Jobscan. (n.d.). *Optimize your resume for applicant tracking systems.* https://www.jobscan.co

Khan Academy. (n.d.). *Free online courses, lessons & practice.* https://www.khanacademy.org

LinkedIn Learning. (n.d.). *Courses taught by industry experts.* https://www.linkedin.com/learning

Microsoft Outlook. (n.d.). *Email, scheduling, and task management tool.* https://outlook.live.com/

Online courses from top institutions. (n.d.). *Coursera.* https://www.coursera.org

Photomath. (n.d.). *Learn math, check homework.* https://photomath.com

RescueTime. (n.d.). *Time management and productivity tracking tool.* https://www.rescuetime.com/

Resumake. (n.d.). *Free resume builder.* https://resumake.io

SaneBox. (n.d.). *Email management tool.* https://www.sanebox.com/

Simply Piano. (n.d.). *Learn piano with a teacher in your pocket.* https://www.joytunes.com/simply-piano

Todoist. (n.d.). *Task management and to-do list app.* https://todoist.com/

Treehouse. (n.d.). *Learn web design, coding, and more.* https://teamtreehouse.com

Trello. (n.d.). *Visual project management tool.* https://trello.com/

x.ai. (n.d.). *AI-powered personal assistant for scheduling.* https://x.ai/

Yummly. (n.d.). *Recipe discovery and meal planner.* https://www.yummly.com

Amanda Fleish

APPENDIX D

AI TOOL EXPLORATION WORKSHEET

Instructions:
Use this worksheet daily. Pick one AI tool from this book or another source. Use it for a few days, then complete this worksheet.

- **Tool Name:** _____

- **Purpose of the Tool:** _____

- **How easy was it to use?** (Rate 1-5) _____

- **What I liked:** _____

- **What I didn't like** _____

- **Would I use it regularly? Why or why not?** _____

APPENDIX E

AI FOR BEGINNERS: 7-DAY CHALLENGE

Instructions:
Complete one AI-related activity per day to ease into using AI in everyday life.

Day 1: Use a voice assistant (Alexa, Siri, Google Assistant) to set a reminder or ask a question.

Day 2: Try an AI-powered writing tool like Grammarly or ChatGPT to improve an email or blog post.

Day 3: Use an AI productivity tool, like Google Calendar's intelligent scheduling or an AI-powered to-do list.

Day 4: Explore an AI-generated recommendation (Netflix, Spotify, or YouTube) and reflect on its accuracy.

Day 5: Test an AI-powered financial tool like Mint or YNAB to analyze your spending habits.

Day 6: Try an AI art or music tool (DALL·E for image generation or Boomy for music creation).

Day 7: Reflect—Which AI tools were the most helpful? Which would you continue using?

APPENDIX F

AI FOR PRODUCTIVITY CHECKLIST

AI can help automate repetitive tasks, improve efficiency, and reduce workload. This checklist will guide you through practical ways to integrate AI into your daily routine.

Organize Your Daily Tasks with AI

AI-powered task managers and planners help keep track of your schedule, deadlines, and essential to-dos.

Try an AI To-Do List App (like Todoist AI, Notion AI, or Microsoft To-Do)

- Add reminders and deadlines for important tasks.

- Let AI prioritize tasks based on urgency and importance.

- Use AI to suggest the best time to complete tasks based on your schedule.

Use AI for Smart Scheduling

- Try AI-powered calendar tools (Google Calendar's intelligent scheduling, Reclaim AI, Motion) to auto-schedule meetings and focus time.

- Allow AI to suggest the best meeting times based on availability.

Automate Emails & Communication

AI can help you write emails faster, respond to messages, and manage your inbox efficiently.

Use AI Writing Assistants for Emails

- Try Grammarly AI or ChatGPT to write and proofread professional emails.

- Use AI to generate quick replies for common email requests.

Declutter Your Inbox with AI

- Enable Gmail's Smart Reply & Smart Compose to speed up responses.

- Use SaneBox or Clean Email to filter and organize emails automatically.

Speed Up Writing & Content Creation

AI can help you write reports, blog posts, social media content, and presentations faster.

Use AI-Powered Writing Tools

- Try ChatGPT, Jasper AI, or Copy.ai to brainstorm and draft content.

- Use Grammarly AI to improve grammar, tone, and clarity.

Enhance Presentations & Reports with AI

- Use Canva AI to design professional slides in minutes.

- Try Notion AI to summarize meeting notes and organize documents.

Save Time with AI-Powered Research & Learning

AI can find information, summarize articles, and help with research projects much faster than traditional methods.

Try AI Research Tools

- Use Elicit AI to summarize research papers and academic articles.

- Ask Perplexity AI or ChatGPT to explain complex topics in simple terms.

Use AI for Learning & Personal Development

- Try Duolingo AI to learn new languages with personalized lessons.

- Use Khan Academy AI Tutor for step-by-step explanations on complex subjects.

Automate Repetitive Tasks & Workflows

AI can eliminate repetitive manual work by automating processes.

Use AI for Workflow Automation

- Try Zapier or IFTTT to connect apps and automate tasks (e.g., saving email attachments to Google Drive).

- Use AI transcription tools like Otter.ai or Descript to transcribe meeting notes automatically.

Set Up AI-Powered Reminders & Notifications

- Enable AI-powered reminders (Google Assistant, Siri, Alexa) for essential deadlines.

- Use AI auto-responses for frequently asked questions in customer service.

Use AI to Manage Your Finances & Save Time on Budgeting

AI-powered finance tools can track expenses, automate budgeting, and find savings opportunities.

Try an AI Finance Assistant

- Use Mint, Cleo, or YNAB AI to monitor spending and suggest budget improvements.

- Let AI analyze your subscriptions and cancel the ones you no longer need.

Automate Financial Planning

- Set up AI alerts for bill due dates and spending limits.

- Use AI-powered investment tools (Wealthfront, Betterment) to grow savings.

AI isn't here to replace you but to help you work smarter!

APPENDIX G

AI PRIVACY AND SAFETY CHECKLIST

Protect Your Online Accounts

- Use Two-Factor Authentication (2FA) – This adds an extra layer of security to your accounts by requiring a code from your phone or email before logging in.

- Create Strong, Unique Passwords—Instead of reusing the same password, use a password manager (like 1Password or LastPass) to generate and store complex passwords.

- Check Your AI App Settings – Many AI tools track user data. Look for privacy settings and limit data sharing where possible.

Be Cautious with AI Chatbots

- Don't Share Personal or Sensitive Information – AI chatbots (like ChatGPT or customer service bots) store conversations. Avoid sharing private details like credit card numbers or passwords.

- Understand What AI Can See – AI tools analyze documents, emails, and messages. Before granting access, double-check what data you are sharing.

Avoid AI-Generated Scams & Deepfakes

- Watch out for Fake Emails and messages. Scammers now use AI-generated phishing emails that look real. If an email asks for personal info or money, verify it's legitimate before clicking links.

- Beware of Deepfakes—AI can create fake images, videos, and voice recordings that look and sound real. If something seems too good to be true, verify the source.

Keep Your Devices & AI Tools Updated

- Install Security Updates—Update your computer, phone, and apps to protect against new AI-driven cyber threats.

- Use AI Security Features—Some AI security tools, like Bitdefender AI or Norton AI Security, automatically detect suspicious activity. Consider using them for extra protection.

Why This Checklist Matters

Many people use AI without realizing how much personal data is being collected.

This checklist helps them:

- Use AI safely while enjoying its benefits.

- Avoid scams and privacy risks when interacting with AI.

- Stay informed about AI-driven security threats.

GLOSSARY OF AI TERMS (SIMPLIFIED)

Artificial Intelligence (AI) – The ability of computers to perform tasks that usually require human intelligence, like learning and problem-solving.

Machine Learning (ML) – A type of AI that learns from data and improves over time without needing to be explicitly programmed.

Deep Learning – A more advanced type of machine learning that mimics how the human brain processes information.

Neural Network – A computer system modeled after the human brain that helps AI recognize patterns in data.

Natural Language Processing (NLP) – The ability of AI to understand and generate human language (e.g., Siri, ChatGPT).

Chatbot – An AI program designed to simulate conversation with humans (e.g., customer service bots).

Generative AI – AI that creates new content, such as text, music, and images (e.g., DALL·E, ChatGPT).

Automation – AI-powered systems that handle repetitive tasks like email sorting or scheduling meetings.

ABOUT THE AUTHOR

Amanda Fleish is an AI enthusiast dedicated to making technology simple and accessible for everyone. She understands the challenges beginners face when navigating the rapidly evolving world of artificial intelligence.

Amanda's mission is to break down complex topics into clear, easy-to-understand concepts, helping non-techie readers feel confident about using AI in their everyday lives. In **Non-Techie Guide to Artificial Intelligence: Breaking Down AI for Beginners,** she provides a friendly, practical approach to AI—free of overwhelming jargon—so anyone can learn how to benefit from this incredible technology.

Amanda continues exploring ways AI can enhance learning, productivity, and creativity when she's not writing.

Continue learning with Amanda's book, **No Tech Skills? No Problem! AI Powered Passive Income: Step-by-Step Strategies to Automate Financial Freedom.**

www.ingramcontent.com/pod-product-compliance
Lightning Source LLC
LaVergne TN
LVHW052304060326
832902LV00021B/3693